SEA LIFE

SHARKS

Edited by Jared Siemens

LIGHTBOX

Go to
www.openlightbox.com,
and enter this book's
unique code.

ACCESS CODE

LBY49567

Lightbox is an all-inclusive digital solution for the teaching and learning of curriculum topics in an original, groundbreaking way. Lightbox is based on National Curriculum Standards.

OPTIMIZED FOR
- ✓ TABLETS
- ✓ WHITEBOARDS
- ✓ COMPUTERS
- ✓ AND MUCH MORE!

Copyright © 2016 Smartbook Media Inc. All rights reserved.

STANDARD FEATURES OF LIGHTBOX

 AUDIO High-quality narration using text-to-speech system

 VIDEOS Embedded high-definition video clips

 ACTIVITIES Printable PDFs that can be emailed and graded

 WEBLINKS Curated links to external, child-safe resources

 SLIDESHOWS Pictorial overviews of key concepts

 INTERACTIVE MAPS Interactive maps and aerial satellite imagery

 QUIZZES Ten multiple choice questions that are automatically graded and emailed for teacher assessment

 KEY WORDS Matching key concepts to their definitions

VIDEOS

WEBLINKS

SLIDESHOWS

QUIZZES
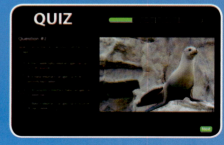

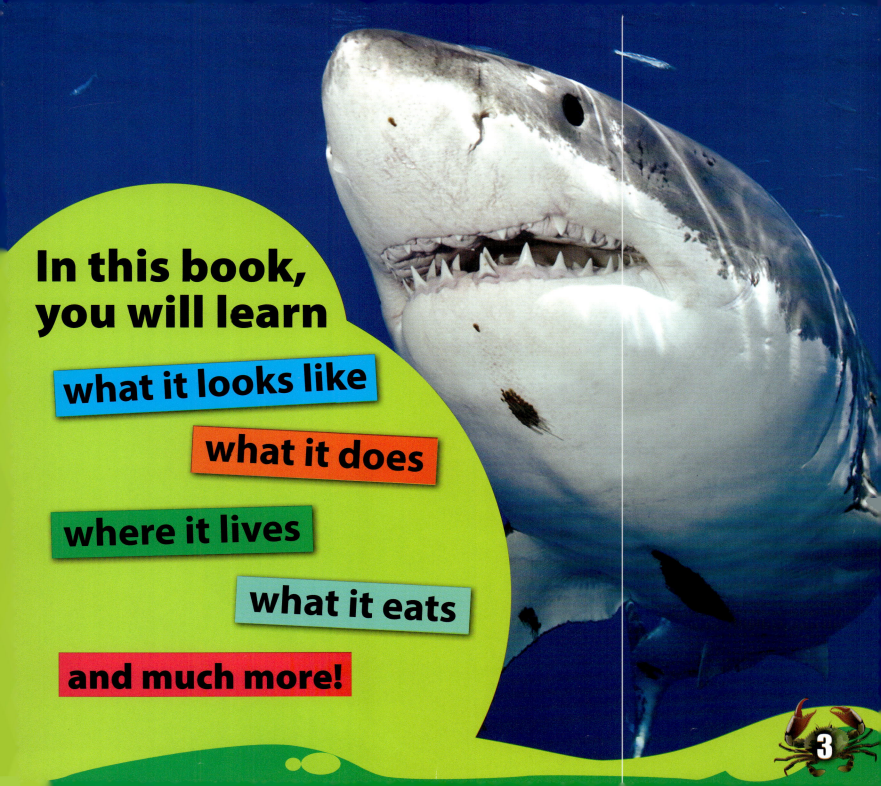

In this book, you will learn

what it looks like

what it does

where it lives

what it eats

and much more!

A shark is a kind of fish that lives in every ocean on Earth.

4

Sharks are the greatest hunters in the ocean.

The coasts of Florida are home to many kinds of sharks.

Many sharks hunt in groups.

They work as a team to catch their food.

Sharks mostly eat fish and other animals.

A great white shark can eat about 11 tons of food each year.

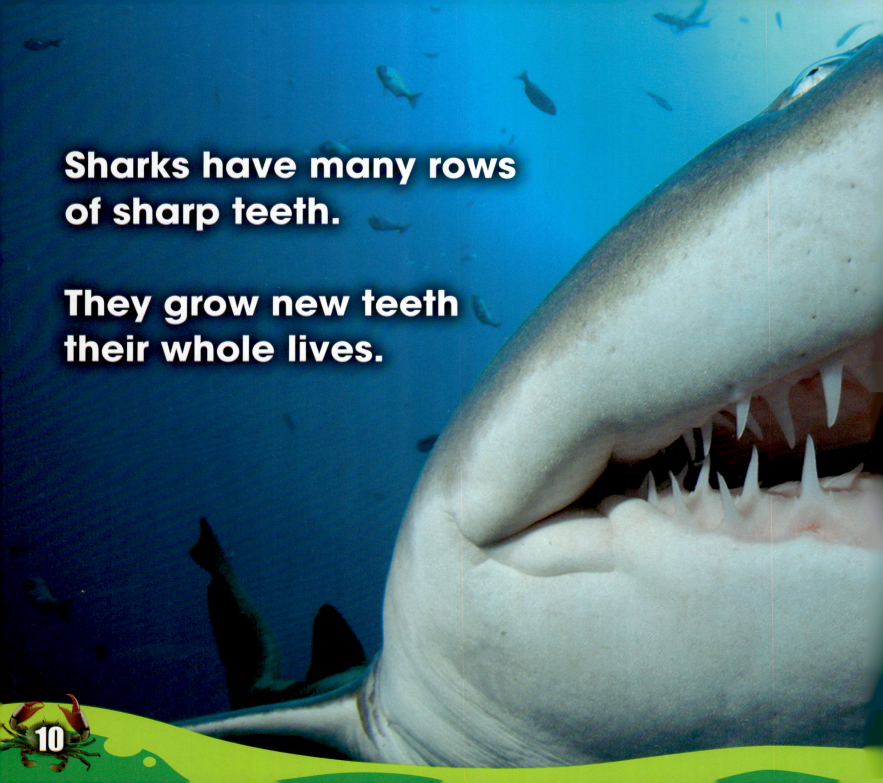

Sharks have many rows of sharp teeth.

They grow new teeth their whole lives.

Sharks can smell under the water.

A shark can smell blood in the water up to 3 miles away.

Sharks do not have bones like other fish.

This makes them very good swimmers.

Sharks can breathe underwater.

They have special lungs
that take air from the water.

There are more than 450 kinds of sharks.

The whale shark is the biggest fish in the world.

The dwarf lantern shark can fit in the palm of a person's hand.

Fishers catch 100,000,000 sharks every year.

SHARK FACTS

These pages provide detailed information that expands on the interesting facts found in the book. They are intended to be used by adults as a learning support to help young readers round out their knowledge of each amazing animal featured in the *Sea Life* series.

Pages 4–5

A shark is a kind of fish that lives in every ocean on Earth. Sharks are the greatest hunters in the ocean. There are more than 400 species of shark currently in the world's oceans. Sharks have been on Earth since the days of the dinosaurs, and have adapted to every marine environment. One of sharks' many adaptations is the ability to sense small electrical signals from other living things. This may give them a considerable advantage when hunting live prey at close range.

Pages 6–7

Many sharks hunt in groups. They work as a team to catch their food. The great white shark is one of the greatest hunters on Earth. Groups of great white sharks will work together and surround an entire school of small fish at once. After they have surrounded the school from all sides, they will attack in unison. Great white sharks hunt seals and other prey in this strategic manner as well.

Pages 8–9

Sharks mostly eat fish and other animals. Shark feeding habits vary from species to species. The whale shark feeds by pulling large amounts of water into its enormous mouth and using its gills like a strainer to filter plankton from the water. Great white sharks will eat almost anything. Most of the time they eat small fish that swim around reefs in the shallow parts of the ocean. Other times, great white sharks will go after larger sea mammals, such as sea lions, small whales, or sea otters. Great white sharks also scavenge and eat dead animals.

Pages 10–11

Sharks have many rows of sharp teeth. They grow new teeth their whole lives. Great white sharks have 24 sharp front teeth that they use for tearing meat. Behind these front teeth, they have another five rows of teeth that are always growing and replacing lost teeth. This means that a great white shark will usually have more than 100 teeth in its mouth.

Pages 12–13  **Sharks can smell under the water.** Sharks do not use their nostrils to breathe. The nostrils are there for the sole purpose of smelling. Their incredible smelling skills help them catch prey. For example, a lemon shark can smell a tuna fish across the length of an Olympic-sized swimming pool.

Pages 14–15  **Sharks do not have bones like other fish. This makes them very good swimmers.** A shark's body is very flexible because it does not have bones. Instead, it has strong cartilage that gives its body structure. This is the same material that makes up human noses and ears. Cartilage gives a shark's body strength, but also allows it to move nimbly through a reef to catch its prey.

Pages 16–17  **Sharks can breathe underwater. They have special lungs that take air from the water.** Sharks, like all other fish in the ocean, can breathe underwater. Sharks use their gills, which are located on the sides of their heads, to take oxygen from the water. Water is pushed into their gills as the shark swims forward with its mouth open. If a shark stops swimming, it will drown.

Pages 18–19  **There are more than 450 kinds of sharks. The whale shark is the biggest fish in the world.** Every species of shark is unique, and varies greatly in size, shape, and appearance. The great white shark has a long, mostly gray-colored body and a white nose. On the other hand, the hammerhead shark has a wide head shaped like a hammer.

Pages 20–21  **Fishers catch 100,000,000 sharks every year.** Some countries around the world catch sharks to eat. Many species of shark are endangered because so many sharks are killed each year. It takes a long time for shark populations to recover from overhunting, because sharks do not have many offspring. If this trend continues, many species of sharks will be in danger of going extinct.

KEY WORDS

Research has shown that as much as 65 percent of all written material published in English is made up of 300 words. These 300 words cannot be taught using pictures or learned by sounding them out. They must be recognized by sight. This book contains 55 common sight words to help young readers improve their reading fluency and comprehension. This book also teaches young readers several important content words, such as proper nouns. These words are paired with pictures to aid in learning and improve understanding.

Page	Sight Words First Appearance
4	a, Earth, every, in, is, kind, lives, of, on, that
5	are, home, many, the, to
6	as, food, group, their, they, work
8	and, animals, eat, other
9	about, can, each, great, white, year
10	grow, have, new
12	under, water
13	away, miles, up
14	do, good, like, makes, not, them, this, very
16	air, from, take
18	more, than, there, world
19	hand

Page	Content Words First Appearance
4	fish, ocean, shark
5	coasts, Florida, hunters
6	team
9	great white shark
10	teeth
13	blood
14	bones, swimmers
16	lungs, underwater
18	whale shark
19	dwarf lantern shark, palm
20	fishers

Published by Smartbook Media Inc.
350 5th Avenue, 59th Floor New York, NY 10118
Website: www.openlightbox.com

Copyright © 2016 Smartbook Media Inc.
All rights reserved. No part of this publication may be reproduced, stored in a retrieval system, or transmitted in any form or by any means, electronic, mechanical, photocopying, recording, or otherwise, without the prior written permission of the publisher.

Library of Congress Control Number: 2015941949

ISBN 978-1-5105-0164-5 (hardcover)
ISBN 978-1-5105-0165-2 (multi-user eBook)

Printed in the United States of America in Brainerd, Minnesota
1 2 3 4 5 6 7 8 9 0   19 18 17 16 15

062015
250515

Project Coordinator: Jared Siemens
Art Director: Terry Paulhus

Every reasonable effort has been made to trace ownership and to obtain permission to reprint copyright material. The publisher would be pleased to have any errors or omissions brought to its attention so that they may be corrected in subsequent printings.

The publisher acknowledges Getty Images and iStock as its primary image suppliers for this title.